Original title:
Love Healed Me

Copyright © 2024 Swan Charm
All rights reserved.

Author: Kene Elistrand
ISBN HARDBACK: 978-9916-89-670-9
ISBN PAPERBACK: 978-9916-89-671-6
ISBN EBOOK: 978-9916-89-672-3

Sails Set Toward New Horizons

With sails unfurled, we leave the shore,
The winds of change call us to explore.
Beneath the sky, so vast and blue,
We chase the dreams we long to pursue.

The waves may crash, the storm may roar,
But in our hearts, we seek for more.
Each gust of wind, a whispering voice,
On this journey, we find our choice.

The stars above guide our way,
Night turns to dawn, and night to day.
With every mile, new tales will grow,
In distant lands, our spirits glow.

Through trials faced and lessons learned,
In every loss, a fire burned.
With courage strong, we'll never tire,
Our deepest hopes will take us higher.

As horizons stretch and shapes align,
We seek the treasures, yours and mine.
With every heartbeat, every breath,
We sail anew, defying death.

Seasons of Healing Blossoming

In spring's embrace, new blooms arise,
Gentle whispers under endless skies.
Each petal softens weary hearts,
Rebirth and hope, where life restarts.

Summer sun brings warmth and light,
Illuminating shadows, chasing night.
With every laugh, we sow the seeds,
In gardens wild, where love proceeds.

Autumn's gold, a time to reflect,
As leaves fall gently, we reconnect.
The winds of change, a subtle call,
In letting go, we find it all.

Winter's stillness teaches rest,
In silence we find our true quest.
Healing comes in the cold and dark,
A flicker of hope, a tiny spark.

Bridges Built with Gentleness

Across the river, we lay our hearts,
With every word, a connection starts.
Gentle hands, so soft and kind,
In building bonds, warmth we find.

With patience strong, we pave the way,
Voices soothing, like a warm ray.
Each step taken, a vow to keep,
In every promise, our trust runs deep.

The arches rise with laughter's grace,
In every challenge, we find our place.
Where storms may rage, we hold on tight,
Together we shine, the guiding light.

When bridges sway, we stand as one,
Through thick and thin, until it's done.
With gentleness, our bonds will thrive,
In kindness, truly, we come alive.

Retold Stories of Brokenness

In fragments scattered, tales are spun,
Each broken piece tells what's begun.
With voice unsteady, we share our pain,
For in the cracks, the light does rain.

The shadows whisper, secrets held,
In vulnerability, our hearts are welded.
From ashes rise, the phoenix sings,
In brokenness, so much life brings.

We gather close, our stories meet,
Finding strength in what's incomplete.
Through shared confessions, we mend the tears,
Binding the wounds with love and cares.

In retelling, we find our grace,
Within the hurt, a sacred space.
From scars we wear, new paths we trace,
Retold, reborn, we embrace.

The Map to Rediscovered Joy

Once lost, now found, a path unfolds,
With every step, a tale retold.
Rough edges smoothed by laughter's call,
In vibrant colors, we stand tall.

Through valleys low and mountains high,
We chart our course beneath the sky.
With compass hearts, we seek the light,
In gentle moments, pure delight.

Each twist and turn a lesson learned,
As fire within us brightly burned.
With open arms, we greet each day,
In tiny joys, we find our way.

In rediscovery, we find the key,
Unlocking doors to wild and free.
The map we carry is made of dreams,
Through joy's adventure, life redeems.

The Comfort of Gentle Hands

In twilight's hush, soft whispers flow,
A touch that heals, a heart aglow.
Each finger dances, weaving dreams,
A balm of peace, or so it seems.

Kindness spills from hands so wide,
In every grasp, love does abide.
Through trials faced, a steady guide,
In gentle strength, we find our stride.

A Symphony of Warm Embraces

The world feels heavy, shadows loom,
Yet in your arms, there's sweet perfume.
A melody sung in silent grace,
Where warmth unfolds, and time finds space.

Each hug a promise, tender, true,
An echo of love, renewed by you.
In every squeeze, a world we share,
A symphony crafted, beyond compare.

Wrapped in the Folds of Compassion

With open hearts, we gather near,
In folds of care, we conquer fear.
Compassion weaves its gentle thread,
A tapestry where love is fed.

In every tear, a story told,
In every smile, a warmth to hold.
We find our strength in hands entwined,
In this embrace, true hope defined.

Grace Found in Simple Moments

In coffee steams and morning light,
In laughter shared, with pure delight.
A fleeting glance, a hand held tight,
In simple moments, hearts take flight.

A sunset's glow, a whispered sigh,
In quiet times, our spirits fly.
Each passing second, a treasure rare,
In life's embrace, we find our care.

Whispers of the Heart

In quiet corners, secrets dwell,
Echoes of dreams, a gentle spell.
Softly spoken, thoughts unfold,
A tale of love, forever told.

With every heartbeat, whispers sigh,
Beneath the stars, where wishes lie.
In tender glances, stories bloom,
A dance of light within the gloom.

Through shadowed paths, we find our way,
Guided by hope, come what may.
In every pause, a promise thrums,
The melody of when love comes.

With fragile strength, we take a stand,
Two souls entwined, a gentle hand.
In laughter's grace, in sorrow's tear,
The whispers echo, always near.

Embracing the Light

Upon the dawn, a new day breaks,
With golden rays, the darkness shakes.
Embrace the warmth, let worries fade,
In every moment, memories made.

The sun ascends with gentle grace,
Illuminates the world's embrace.
With open hearts, we share the glow,
And in the light, our spirits grow.

Through waves of color, hope ignites,
A tapestry of vibrant sights.
In laughter shared and kindness shown,
We find the love we've always known.

Each twinkling star, a wish to claim,
In unity, we're never the same.
Together we shine, spirits bright,
As we dance beneath the enveloping light.

When Shadows Fade

When twilight falls, the shadows play,
In whispered tones, they drift away.
The night reveals what once was veiled,
In gentle peace, our hearts are healed.

Each star a beacon, shining clear,
Guiding our dreams, dispelling fear.
In silver whispers, truths unwind,
The essence of love, so hard to find.

With every breath, we shed the past,
Embracing moments that forever last.
When shadows fade, the light breaks through,
And in that space, we start anew.

Let echoes linger, stories weave,
As dawn arrives, we come to believe.
In the warmth of day, all will mend,
When shadows fade, our spirits blend.

A Touch Beyond Time

In the stillness, we find our place,
A timeless dance, a soft embrace.
With every heartbeat, history calls,
Through endless moments, love enthralls.

In faded pages, stories lie,
Whispers of dreams that never die.
A touch beyond what eyes can see,
Connected souls, you and me.

Through swirling winds, our voices blend,
In timeless realms where echoes send.
With every gaze, a silent vow,
Together forged, from then to now.

In twilight's glow, we come alive,
With every heartbeat, we survive.
A touch beyond, where moments gleam,
In the dance of life, we find our dream.

Circles of Resilient Hearts

In twilight's glow, we gather near,
With whispers soft, we banish fear.
A bond unbroken, forged in night,
Together strong, we seek the light.

Through storms and trials, we will stand,
United souls, both brave and grand.
With arms entwined, we face the day,
Our hearts the compass, guiding our way.

Each setback met with fierce embrace,
A circle drawn, a sacred space.
For in our hearts, resilience lies,
A spark that leaps and never dies.

Through laughter shared and tears we weep,
In circles wide, our promises keep.
A tapestry of stories spun,
In every heart, a battle won.

So let us celebrate this dance,
In every glance, a second chance.
Forever bound, we rise and stand,
In circles of a steadfast land.

The Canvas of Enduring Affection

Brush strokes blend in colors bright,
A canvas drawn in morning light.
Each layer rich with hopes and dreams,
As life unfolds, it softly gleams.

In shades of orange, blue, and gold,
Enduring tales of love retold.
With every hue, our stories blend,
A masterpiece that never ends.

Gentle hands create and dare,
With whispers sweet, we show we care.
Each line a promise, bold and true,
In every shade, my heart is you.

Like vibrant flowers that reach for skies,
Our love, a claim that never dies.
Together, we reshape the frame,
In this grand work, we forge the same.

So let us paint with all our heart,
In every day, a brand new start.
For on this canvas, wide and vast,
Enduring love will hold us fast.

Stitches of Time and Care

With needle fine and thread of gold,
We weave our stories, strong and bold.
Each stitch a moment, soft and true,
A tapestry of me and you.

In patchwork bright, our lives entwine,
With memories stitched, your hand in mine.
Through seasons change, we stand prepared,
In every square, the love we shared.

Through frays and knots, we gently mend,
A fabric rich, we will defend.
With every loop, our hopes restore,
Together, we can weather more.

So gather close, let hearts embrace,
The warmth of love, our sacred space.
In stitches tight, we find our peace,
With every thread, our joys increase.

As time unravels, we remain,
Each stitch a link in joy and pain.
With courage sewn in every seam,
We craft our lives, a cherished dream.

Glimpses of a Gentle Horizon

In softest hues, the dawn awakes,
A gentle breeze, the morning breaks.
With every step, we trace the line,
Where sky and earth in beauty twine.

The horizon whispers tales untold,
Of dreams ignited, hearts made bold.
With every glance beyond the shore,
We find the peace we're searching for.

In quiet moments, shadows fade,
As daylight paints a grand parade.
We seek the paths where hope remains,
In glowing hues, it banishes pains.

So let us walk in light's embrace,
With every heartbeat, find our place.
In glimpses of the day's debut,
Together, we will start anew.

And as the stars begin to sway,
We hold the night and shape the day.
For in this dance of light and love,
We find our dreams, like stars above.

Kindgestures That Are Eternal

A smile shared on a rainy day,
A hand reached out, a warm display.
In quiet moments, kindness grows,
A seed of hope that softly glows.

A simple word, a glance that cares,
In laughter shared, the burden bears.
A gentle touch, a thoughtful deed,
The warmth within, a silent creed.

In times of need, a heart so near,
With every hug, it draws us clear.
Connections forged in light and grace,
In these small acts, we find our place.

Through years that pass, these gestures stay,
A light that guides us on our way.
For kindness lingers, never fades,
In every heart, its mark pervades.

Eternal bonds through simple ways,
In small gestures, love always plays.
And when we part, the echoes ring,
In kindness shared, our voices sing.

Heartbeats in Perfect Harmony

Two souls entwined in gentle flow,
In rhythms soft, their feelings grow.
Each glance a note, each touch a song,
Together where they both belong.

A laughter shared, a tear that slips,
In quiet moments, love's sweet scripts.
Two hearts a-dance, in sync, they sway,
A melody that guides the way.

In whispered dreams beneath the stars,
They find their peace, despite the scars.
With every heartbeat, they embrace,
A symphony in time and space.

Through trials faced and joys embraced,
In love's warm fold, they find their place.
With every breath, their souls align,
As heartbeats echo, soft and fine.

In perfect harmony, they stand,
Together, strong, hand in hand.
For love, a song that never dies,
In heartbeats shared, the truth lies.

Resting in Radiant Kindness

In gentle arms, we find our peace,
A sanctuary where cares cease.
With every hug, the world feels light,
A warmth that glows, a sweet delight.

The kindness shared in smiles so bright,
A soothing balm in darkest night.
In tender words that softly flow,
A garden where warm feelings grow.

With every laugh, the heart expands,
In shared moments, life understands.
Together resting, side by side,
In kindness wrapped, our hearts abide.

When storms arise, we face them strong,
In radiant warmth, we sing our song.
For love bestowed through gentle grace,
Gives us courage, a sacred space.

In every shared serene embrace,
Kindness lingers, time can't erase.
In resting hearts, our spirits mend,
A radiant bond that will not end.

A Quilt of Shared Sorrows

In patches sewn from tears and smiles,
We wrap our hearts in tender miles.
Each story told, a thread that's spun,
A quilt of sorrows, shared as one.

With every stitch, a memory held,
In whispered pain, our hope dispelled.
Together brave, through trials we roam,
In woven love, we find our home.

With hands that tremble, hearts laid bare,
In each embrace, a light we share.
For every burden, lightened grace,
In sorrow's quilt, we find our place.

Through frayed edges, strength emerges,
In whispered lore, our spirit surges.
As we recount the nights of fear,
A testament to those we hold dear.

So let us weave with colors bright,
A tapestry of shared delight.
For in our sorrows, joy we find,
A quilt of love, forever kind.

Threads of Understanding

In whispers soft, we share our fears,
A tapestry woven through the years.
Each thread a voice, a heart, a song,
Together we stand, united, strong.

Through kindness sown, we plant the seeds,
Of trust and hope, fulfilling needs.
We unravel doubts, weave in the light,
A guiding force through darkest night.

The colors blend, revealing grace,
In every heart, a sacred space.
As time unfolds, the fabric grows,
Threads of love, as true friendship shows.

Hand in hand, we bridge the gaps,
With open hearts, the world adapts.
In every stitch, a promise made,
Together, we rise, unafraid.

So let us weave with gentle hands,
A world transformed where kindness stands.
Through threads of understanding, we find,
A brighter path for all mankind.

The Garden of Renewal

In the quiet soil, our dreams take root,
Beneath the sun, we gently shoot.
With every rain, our spirits grow,
In this garden, love will flow.

Seeds of hope in rows align,
With patience, they flourish, intertwine.
We nurture blooms with tender care,
In every petal, life laid bare.

Nature whispers, secrets unfold,
Stories of warmth, of brave and bold.
In vibrant colors, we see the proof,
Life's beautiful cycle, a joyful truth.

Through seasons changing, we understand,
In the dance of time, we take a stand.
Rebirth occurs in every hue,
In this garden, we're born anew.

So plant your dreams, let them expand,
A sanctuary where life is planned.
In the garden of renewal, we thrive,
Where every soul is free to strive.

Reaching for Tomorrow

With open arms, we grasp the dawn,
Embracing change, our fears withdrawn.
A future bright, within our sight,
We kindle hope, ignite the light.

Each step we take, a journey grand,
In unity, together we stand.
With courage found, we rise above,
For every soul, a chance to love.

The road ahead may twist and turn,
Yet in our hearts, the fire will burn.
With dreams alight, we pave the way,
Reaching for tomorrow, come what may.

Through shadows cast, we find our way,
In every challenge, brighter days.
With every heartbeat, a promise made,
Together we shine, unafraid.

So let us chase the stars that gleam,
And build a world where hope's the theme.
Reaching for tomorrow, hand in hand,
A brighter future, we will stand.

A Dance of Empathy

In the stillness, we take our place,
With open hearts, we find the space.
A gentle sway, a tender touch,
In this dance, we feel so much.

Each step a rhythm, a heartbeat shared,
A chorus of souls that truly cared.
In every glance, a silent vow,
To lift each other, here and now.

With every turn, we learn to see,
The beauty in our shared journey.
Through tears and laughter, we intertwine,
In this dance of empathy, we shine.

So take my hand, let's join the flow,
In this sacred space, together we grow.
With every pirouette, we build the bridge,
Over walls that once made us cringe.

Through movements soft, our souls unite,
In understanding, we find our light.
The dance goes on, a glorious song,
In empathy's embrace, we all belong.

From Ashes to Anew

From ashes cold, new life will rise,
Hope glimmers faint, beneath dark skies.
The past is gone, a whisper's haze,
Embrace the dawn, and brighter days.

With every breath, we start again,
A journey forged from loss and pain.
The heart reborn in sacred flame,
We write our stories, none the same.

Through trials faced, we learn to stand,
Together strong, we share this land.
With every step, a choice we make,
For in the fire, the soul won't break.

The scars we bear, a badge of pride,
In unity, we will abide.
From ashes high, the spirit sings,
A world renewed, on hope's soft wings.

So let us dance beneath the light,
A tapestry of dark and bright.
From ashes deep, we rise anew,
With open hearts, we will pursue.

The Lantern of Shared Light

In darkest nights, we find a flame,
A lantern bright, we call by name.
Together we shine, through joy and strife,
In every heart, we share this life.

Hand in hand, with light we share,
A guiding glow, we find our care.
Through every trial, together bend,
Our shared light whispers, love won't end.

When shadows fall, and hope seems dim,
Our lantern's glow will never slim.
For in each spark, there lies a thread,
A bond of love that can't be shed.

Through every storm, we hold on tight,
With open eyes, we face the night.
The lantern shines, a beacon clear,
In shared light's warmth, we lose our fear.

So lift your heart to skies above,
With every laugh, we weave our love.
Together we walk, in joyous flight,
Our journey bright, by shared light.

Heartstrings Tuning to Serenity

In quiet moments, we find our tune,
Soft melodies beneath the moon.
With gentle breaths, we intertwine,
In heartstrings' pull, our souls align.

A symphony of whispered peace,
In every note, our worries cease.
Harmony flows, both near and far,
Guiding us home, like a distant star.

With every thrum, the world does fade,
In stillness finds the love we've made.
Each beat a prayer, a sacred bond,
In this sweet silence, we respond.

As seasons shift, we learn to grow,
Through all we face, our hearts will know.
In gentle strums, we find our way,
Through heartstrings' tune, come what may.

So let us breathe, both near and wide,
In tranquil notes, we shall abide.
With every song, our spirits free,
We find our peace in harmony.

Rebirth Beneath the Stars

Beneath the stars, a tale unfolds,
Of dreams once lost and hearts retold.
In cosmic light, we seek our place,
A journey spun through time and space.

Each twinkling light, a wish anew,
A beckoning call to those who pursue.
With open hearts, we gaze and yearn,
For in the dark, the fire will burn.

Through shadowed paths, we rise and soar,
With every breath, we long for more.
The universe sings, of life's embrace,
In stardust lost, we find our grace.

In every star, a story glows,
Of past and future, ebb and flows.
Rebirth awaits, in night's embrace,
Together strong, we'll find our space.

So let us dream 'neath endless skies,
For every end, a new arise.
Rebirth beneath the stars up high,
A cosmic dance, our spirits fly.

A Tapestry of Unison

In colors bright, threads entwine,
Each story told, a path divine.
Harmony weaves through every seam,
A dance of light, a shared dream.

Voices blend, a gentle hum,
Together strong, a beating drum.
In woven hearts, the hope we find,
A tapestry of the intertwined.

With hands that mold, we shape our fate,
In whispered vows, we contemplate.
Each stitch a bond, a tale to share,
In unison, we rise and dare.

Through stormy seas and tranquil days,
We find our way through love's array.
In every thread, a story flows,
A tapestry where friendship grows.

So let us weave, hand in hand,
A vibrant cloth across the land.
In every fold, hope will abide,
A tapestry, our hearts as guide.

The Resounding Reunion

In twilight's glow, the echoes play,
Old friends appear, come what may.
Laughter bounces, memories spry,
Under the vast, embracing sky.

From distant lands, our paths converge,
Around the fire, our spirits surge.
Tales of heartache, joy, and grace,
In every word, a warm embrace.

The night unfolds, stars watch anew,
Binding us close, like morning dew.
Each story shared, a spark of light,
In darkness, love keeps us bright.

With every hug, the bonds grow strong,
Together we've weathered, together belong.
In this reunion, time stands still,
In hearts entwined, we find our will.

So let the music play once more,
In every note, the love we store.
A resounding reunion, a dance divine,
In cherished moments, forever we shine.

Whispers of Rebirth

In silent woods, the dawn unfolds,
A story new, the earth beholds.
Soft whispers rise, like gentle rain,
Renewed by hope, we break the chain.

From ashes cold, new life does spring,
In every breath, the joy we bring.
With open hearts, we greet the morn,
In paths of light, our souls reborn.

Each bud that blooms, a promise true,
In nature's dance, we find our cue.
The circle spins, a vibrant flow,
In whispers soft, the new must grow.

From shadows past, we find our way,
In every heart, the light will stay.
Together we rise, hand in hand,
In whispers of rebirth, we stand.

So let the seasons turn and shift,
In every moment, a timeless gift.
Through trials faced, and lessons learned,
In whispers of rebirth, we've yearned.

Embraced by Grace

In gentle arms, the world does sway,
Embraced by grace, we find our way.
Through trials faced, we lift our eyes,
In every fall, the hope will rise.

With every breath, we draw in peace,
In love's sweet song, our fears will cease.
A tender touch, a guiding hand,
In grace, united, together we stand.

The journey's long, but hearts endure,
In moments shared, we find the cure.
With open arms, we face the night,
Embraced by grace, we find our light.

Through endless storms and skies of gray,
With every dawn, we greet the day.
In laughter shared, in tears released,
In grace, our souls are truly ceased.

So let our hearts beat as one,
In every battle fought, we've won.
Embraced by grace, we'll carry forth,
In love's embrace, we find our worth.

From Fractured to Flourishing

In shadows deep where silence dwells,
A whisper blooms, the heart compels.
From shards of glass, new light will weave,
Hope takes root, and we believe.

The cracks once wide, now gently mend,
With every scar, a chance to fend.
The journey tough, yet spirits soar,
From fractured dreams, we build once more.

With every step, a brighter hue,
The past behind, a world anew.
Embracing change, we grow and rise,
In tender light, we touch the skies.

In every struggle, lessons learned,
Through winding paths where courage burned.
The pain transformed, a strength revealed,
In flourishing, our hearts are healed.

Together bound, our spirits dance,
In unity, we take a chance.
From fractured times, a love we find,
In flourishing, we intertwine.

A Tapestry of Unbroken Moments

Threads of time weave bright and bold,
In every loop, a tale unfolds.
A tapestry kissed by the sun,
Unbroken moments, a life begun.

Each stitch a heartbeat, soft and clear,
Memories echo, we hold dear.
The colors vibrant, rich with light,
In woven love, we find our might.

From laughter shared to tears we shed,
In every hue, our stories spread.
These moments gathered, not in vain,
A fabric strong, through joy and pain.

With every thread, a bond we share,
In unbroken ties, love's gentle care.
Together we craft, through day and night,
A tapestry of pure delight.

In every corner of this space,
Our lives entwined, a warm embrace.
A legacy stitched with heart and soul,
In time's sweet dance, we are made whole.

The Bridge of Connection

Beneath the arch of twilight's glow,
A bridge of dreams begins to flow.
Connecting hearts from near to far,
In every step, a guiding star.

With hands outstretched, we find our way,
In whispered words, we choose to stay.
Through laughter shared and sorrow's weight,
On this bridge, we cultivate.

The distance fades when hearts unite,
In shared journeys, we write our flight.
With every word, a seed we plant,
In connection's grace, our spirits chant.

From shores unknown to familiar lands,
In unity, we take our stands.
A link that binds through thick and thin,
The bridge of connection, where we begin.

With open hearts and voices strong,
Together, we belong.
As we traverse, our souls ignite,
On this bridge, we shine so bright.

Rise Like the Phoenix of Affection

From ashes low, a rise, a flare,
With wings of hope, we claim the air.
The phoenix sings a song so sweet,
In love's embrace, our hearts repeat.

With every fall, new strength is born,
In trials faced, we're never torn.
Through flames of doubt, we blaze anew,
In affection's light, our dreams come true.

We spread our wings in colors bright,
In unity, we reach the height.
Together bound, we soar and glide,
With every heartbeat, love is our guide.

Through storms and trials, we find our way,
Emerging strong with each new day.
The phoenix rises, fierce and grace,
In affection's warmth, we find our place.

In endless flight, we'll never tire,
Embraced in love's eternal fire.
From ashes dark to skies above,
We rise like the phoenix of love.

When Warmth Danced Through Shadows

In twilight's gentle embrace,
Where whispers of dreams reside,
The warmth danced through the shadows,
Awakening hearts inside.

Laughter floated on the breeze,
As night fell with a soft sigh,
Stars blinked like secret promises,
In the vast, endless sky.

Footsteps echoed on the path,
Memory's familiar song,
Every moment a cherished gift,
In the night we belong.

Flickering lanterns softly glowed,
Casting hope upon our way,
In the stillness we found solace,
As night melted into day.

Together we wove the stories,
Knit with threads of light and grace,
When warmth danced through the shadows,
We found our sacred space.

Reviving the Spirit Within

In the silence, whispers call,
A gentle breeze stirs the soul,
Awakening fire within us,
Making broken hearts whole.

Through hazy dreams and lost hopes,
The dawn breaks with a new start,
Each breath, a step toward healing,
Reviving the spirit's heart.

Nature sings its sweet ballad,
In colors so rich and bright,
Every petal holds a promise,
Of strength found in the light.

As the sun paints the sky gold,
The shadows begin to fade,
With courage we rise together,
In the warmth, unafraid.

With each challenge, we grow stronger,
Learning to dance through the pain,
Reviving the spirit within us,
In joy, we'll rise again.

Threads of Affection Weaving Hope

In the tapestry of hearts,
Threads of affection intertwine,
Each moment cherished and held,
With laughter as the design.

Through the storms and sunny days,
We cherish what we create,
With love, we sew the fabric,
Our stories, intimate fate.

Woven dreams in vibrant hues,
Map our journey, side by side,
In every stitch a memory,
Binding hearts with love's guide.

As the seasons gently change,
We find solace in our art,
Threads of affection weaving hope,
In every beating heart.

Together we'll face tomorrow,
With courage that brightly glows,
In the quilt of life we find peace,
As love, like a river, flows.

The Healing Touch of Kindred Souls

In the stillness of the night,
Kindred souls draw near with care,
With whispers of understanding,
Their presence light as air.

A soothing balm for weary hearts,
Their laughter like a song,
Each moment spent together,
Reminds us where we belong.

In the depths of shared silence,
Words aren't always needed clear,
The healing touch of friendship,
Wraps our spirits, draws us near.

Through the trials and the triumphs,
United, we cast our fears,
With kindred souls beside us,
We celebrate our tears.

With every heartbeat intertwined,
We find strength in each embrace,
The healing touch of kindred souls,
Creates our sacred space.

A Heart Mended in Grace

In shadows deep, a heart laid bare,
With gentle hands, the healer's care.
With threads of hope and love entwined,
A tapestry of peace defined.

The pain once sharp begins to fade,
In quiet moments, faith is made.
With every stitch, a story grows,
Of battles fought and love's sweet flows.

Embracing warmth, the heart's embrace,
Reclaims the lost and finds its place.
In grace we rise, in light we stand,
Together, dreams in hand we band.

So let the past release its hold,
A brighter path begins to unfold.
In trust we find our spirits soar,
A heart mended, forevermore.

The Rhythm of Second Chances

The ticking clock, a steady sound,
In every beat, new hopes are found.
With whispered dreams that softly call,
We rise again, refusing to fall.

Each stumble brings a lesson clear,
A chance to shed our foolish fear.
Embrace the dance, take one more try,
For every end, there's a new sky.

In fragile hearts, resounding grace,
We learn to trust, we learn to face.
So take my hand, we'll journey wide,
Through valleys low and mountain side.

With every breath, a song we sing,
In harmony, our spirits cling.
The rhythm flows, anew we see,
Second chances set us free.

Blossoms After the Storm

Once fierce and wild, the tempest raged,
In swirling winds, our fears were paged.
Yet after dark, the sun will shine,
And life returns, pure and divine.

With tender care, the earth revives,
The fragrance sweet, as spirit thrives.
In colors bright, our hopes arise,
A canvas painted 'neath wide skies.

Each petal soft, a whispered prayer,
For strength bestowed and love laid bare.
Together we stand, hand in hand,
As blossoms dance upon the land.

From ashes cold, to warmth's embrace,
We rise anew, with boundless grace.
In every bloom, a story shared,
Of love's endurance, truly cared.

Echoes of Unseen Care

In silence deep, where shadows dwell,
There lies a truth we hold so well.
Though unseen hands may gently guide,
The heart will know, the soul abides.

A gentle word, a soft embrace,
Can light a path through darkest space.
With every thought, we're intertwined,
In echoes deep, our love defined.

Through trials faced, and tears we shed,
The threads of care, a tapestry spread.
In whispers heard, and laughter shared,
The bonds of life, forever spared.

So let us cherish those we hold,
In every story shared, retold.
For love unseen, its strength can bear,
The echoes of our unseen care.

Transformed by Tenderness

In gentle whispers, hearts awake,
A fragile bond, no pain can break.
Soft embraces, truth revealed,
In warmth and care, our wounds are healed.

Through kindness wrapped, we find our way,
With every tear, we learn to stay.
The power grows in tender touch,
Together we'll rise, it means so much.

In quiet moments, love ignites,
Setting free our inner sights.
Transcending scars, we gently mend,
With every heartbeat, we're reborn, friend.

A world transformed by simple grace,
In tenderness, we find our place.
United through both joy and strife,
Love guides us through this precious life.

Echoes of Compassion

In shadows cast, a voice will rise,
With quiet strength, it never lies.
Each echo calls, a tender sound,
In every heart, compassion found.

Through open hands, we share our light,
With every act, we unite the fight.
In kindness shared, we grow anew,
A circle strong, with love as glue.

Through pain and strife, let empathy soar,
For in our hearts, compassion's core.
We'll bridge the gaps that time has made,
In echoes sweet, our fears will fade.

With every voice that dares to speak,
In gentle strength, we find the peak.
Together we rise, through thick and thin,
In echoes of love, we learn to begin.

Rising from the Depths

From darkness deep, we find a spark,
A light within, dispelling dark.
With courage born from trials faced,
We rise above, our fears displaced.

Each step we take, a path revealed,
Through storms and doubts, our fate is sealed.
With strength renewed, we push our way,
To greet the dawn of a brighter day.

In unity, our voices blend,
A chorus strong, where hearts extend.
Through every challenge, faith will guide,
In rising tides, we learn to bide.

With hope as fuel, we lift our sight,
From shadows cast, we seek the light.
Transforming pain into our strength,
Together we soar, at any length.

Tides of Rejuvenation

In waves of change, we find our flow,
With every ebb, new wonders grow.
As tides recede, reveal the shore,
In every season, we seek for more.

With every wave, a story told,
Of hearts that soften, of lives enfold.
Through cycles vast, we learn to trust,
In nature's pulse, we find our must.

In quiet moments, breathe anew,
With every dawn, fresh starts ensue.
Embracing all, both joy and pain,
In tides of life, we break each chain.

As waters rise, we lift our hands,
Together standing on shifting sands.
Through storms and calm, we understand,
In tides of love, we make our stand.

Wings of Redemption

In shadows deep, where hope does dwell,
A whispered prayer, a silent bell.
Through storm and strife, I seek to rise,
With outstretched wings beneath the skies.

Each tear I shed, a lesson learned,
With every flame, a heart that burned.
Reclaimed by grace, I find my way,
In light of dawn, I greet the day.

The past a ghost, but not my chain,
In freedom's arms, I'll shed the pain.
With courage fierce, I face the flight,
And gather strength from endless light.

With each new dawn, the skies I grace,
In love's embrace, I find my place.
So spread your wings, let spirits soar,
For in redemption, we're reborn.

A journey long, with lessons blessed,
In truth I rise, my heart at rest.
So take my hand, we'll face the storm,
Together shine, our spirits warm.

Serenade of Souls

In twilight's hush, the stars awake,
A gentle song on breezes break.
Each melody, a heart in tune,
A serenade beneath the moon.

With whispers soft, the night unfolds,
In cryptic tales that love upholds.
Two souls entwined in rhythm sweet,
A dance of hearts, their hearts repeat.

Through valleys deep and mountains high,
The whispers echo, never die.
In sacred notes, our spirits merge,
A timeless bond, we feel the urge.

The music flows like rivers wide,
With every heartbeat, love's tide.
In symphonies that time creates,
We find our peace, where fate awaits.

Together on this path we roam,
Each step, a stitch that weaves our home.
In harmony, our souls unite,
A serenade of purest light.

The Blossoming Path

In gardens rich where flowers bloom,
A path of hope dispels the gloom.
With every step, new dreams arise,
A tapestry beneath the skies.

Each petal soft, a story told,
Of love and courage, bright and bold.
In vibrant hues, the world ignites,
A symphony of soft delights.

With morning's kiss, the dew aligns,
A fragrant breath, a heart that shines.
Through winding ways, we find our grace,
In nature's arms, a warm embrace.

As seasons change, the blooms will fade,
Yet in their wake, new hope is laid.
With open hearts, our spirits thrive,
On blossoming paths, we come alive.

Embrace the journey, trust the flow,
For every step helps us to grow.
In unity, our dreams are sown,
On this path, we're never alone.

Hearts Resilient

In stormy seas, our hearts do face,
The trials that life cannot erase.
With every blow, we bend, not break,
In bonds of love, we find our stake.

Through trials thick and sorrows deep,
Our spirits wake from restless sleep.
With courage stitched in every seam,
We rise anew and dare to dream.

In warmth of trust, we hold our ground,
In whispered hopes, true strength is found.
Through valleys low and peaks so high,
Our hearts resilient touch the sky.

So let the winds of life then blow,
With every gust, our roots will grow.
In unity, we'll face the strife,
For in our hearts, we hold our life.

Together we rise, our spirits soar,
With every challenge, we seek more.
In love's embrace, we find our light,
For hearts resilient shine so bright.

Healing in Your Eyes

In the depths of your gaze, I find,
A solace that eases my mind.
With each whisper, a tender breeze,
Restoring my heart, bringing me peace.

The pain of the past fades away,
In those moments when we sway.
Your kindness, a balm for my soul,
In your presence, I feel whole.

Every tear that cascades down,
Transforms into jewels, no more frown.
Your laughter, a light in the dark,
Guides me back, ignites a spark.

With every glance, a promise made,
To shield me from the world's cascade.
In your world, I long to reside,
Healing blooms with you by my side.

Together we'll chase the night,
Embracing each ray of soft light.
In healing, we find our way,
In your eyes, forever I'll stay.

The Rebirth of Us

Once lost in shadows, we now stand,
Together writing love's new strand.
With each sunrise, a canvas bright,
Painting our dreams in pure delight.

Through storms and trials, we have grown,
In the garden of love, seeds have flown.
Roots intertwine, stronger each day,
Nurtured by hope as we find our way.

In secret whispers, we rebuild,
Promises made, our hearts fulfilled.
With every heartbeat, we ignite,
A flame eternal, warm and bright.

Hand in hand, we brave the night,
No longer blinded, we share the light.
In the echoes of all we've seen,
The rebirth of us, a love serene.

We dance to the rhythm of our song,
In unity, where we belong.
A tapestry woven with trust and grace,
In the rebirth of us, we've found our place.

A Symphony of Restoration

In the stillness, notes begin to play,
A symphony crafting a brand-new day.
Harmonies gentle, a soothing balm,
Restoring our spirits, a sweet calm.

Each chord reverberates, feelings rise,
Painting the sky in vibrant dyes.
A melody penned in the heart's refrain,
Whispers of love that soften the pain.

Through crescendos, we find our way,
In the orchestra of life, we sway.
Together we sing, our voices blend,
A timeless song that will never end.

With every pause, silence speaks bold,
Stories of healing that need to be told.
In this symphony, hope takes flight,
Guiding us gently into the night.

In the echoes, we gather close,
Our hearts aligned, no need for prose.
A symphony crafted in each embrace,
Restoration found in love's true grace.

Guided by Warmth

Under starlit skies, we find our way,
Guided by warmth, come what may.
The night wraps around, so tender and bright,
In your arms, everything feels right.

Soft whispers carried on the breeze,
Memories linger like fading leaves.
With every heartbeat, a safe refrain,
Our love, a shelter, free from pain.

Through life's journey, hand in hand,
In this embrace, we take a stand.
Your laughter ignites a gentle flame,
In this dance of life, we stay the same.

As dawn approaches, dreams unfold,
Each moment cherished, together we hold.
With you beside me, fears dissipate,
Guided by warmth, we celebrate.

In the quiet spaces, truths emerge,
A radiant connection, love's pure surge.
Together forever, our spirits entwined,
Guided by warmth, our souls aligned.

The Gentle Resurgence

In whispers soft, the dawn unfolds,
A tender light on stories told.
From shadows deep, a heart will rise,
To greet the warmth of open skies.

With every ripple, hope takes flight,
As petals bloom in morning light.
The world, it breathes a sacred song,
In nature's arms, we all belong.

The rivers flow with purpose clear,
Their currents wash away our fear.
In gentle waves, new dreams are cast,
A future bright, a shadowed past.

Upon the hills, the flowers sway,
In vibrant hues that chase the gray.
The seasons turn, as time will keep,
Our souls awaken from their sleep.

Through trials faced, a bond we find,
In every heartbeat, so entwined.
The gentle rise, a sweet embrace,
Together we will find our place.

Bonds That Mend

In moments shared, our spirits grow,
Through laughter's light, and tears that flow.
The ties of love, they weave so tight,
In darkest hours, they shine so bright.

With every word, we stitch the seam,
Repairing hearts like a tender dream.
In silent whispers, trust takes shape,
A tapestry that none can break.

Along the road, we walk so near,
Supporting strength, conquering fear.
Through storms we stand, against the tide,
In unity, we take our stride.

As seasons change, our roots grow deep,
In fertile soil, our dreams we keep.
The bonds we share will never fade,
Through time and space, our love cascades.

In every challenge, hand in hand,
Together we will make our stand.
For bonds that mend are made to last,
A future bright, built on the past.

Nourished by Affection

In quiet moments, love's embrace,
A soft caress, a sacred space.
We find our strength in gentle touch,
The warmth of hearts that mean so much.

With every glance, affection grows,
Like blooming flowers, it brightly shows.
In laughter shared, in stories spun,
Our souls entwined, two hearts as one.

A kindness shared, a hand to hold,
In every lesson, dreams unfold.
From simple joys to laughter's song,
In love united, we grow strong.

Through trials faced, we will not part,
For every beat, a shared heart.
In nurturing love, we find our way,
Creating warmth in every day.

With roots of trust, our bonds will thrive,
In this embrace, we come alive.
Nourished by affection's flow,
Together, always, we will grow.

From Ashes to Embrace

In embers lost, a spark is born,
A flicker of hope, where dreams are worn.
From ashes gray, we rise anew,
With open hearts, the world in view.

Through trials faced and battles fought,
In every struggle, wisdom's sought.
With lessons learned, we stand so tall,
United we rise, together we fall.

The past may linger, shadows trace,
Yet light breaks through, a warm embrace.
In every tear, a story's told,
Of strength reborn from embers bold.

With every step, we'll forge ahead,
From whispered fears to words unsaid.
In courage found, our spirits soar,
Embracing life, forever more.

From ashes cold, new flames shall blaze,
Illuminating our winding ways.
A journey shared, a love so bright,
From ashes to embrace, our light.

Mosaic Heartstrings

In every shard of light we find,
A story woven, intertwined.
Each piece a sound, a whispered part,
Together forming a mosaic heart.

Colors clash and gently blend,
A tapestry that has no end.
From fragments lost, new dreams are cast,
A future built, not bound by past.

We dance upon the fractured glass,
Where laughter echoes, and shadows pass.
Embracing flaws, we choose to start,
Forever bound by heart to heart.

Each string a tale of love's embrace,
In harmony, we find our place.
With every note, our souls can sing,
A symphony of everything.

Together we create our song,
A melody that blooms so strong.
In every heartbeat, truths unfold,
The magic of our love retold.

Rewritten Promises

Pages turned and ink runs dry,
Stars realign in the vast sky.
Words once lost, now find a way,
To echo hope in light of day.

Promises made beneath the moon,
Carried softly, like a tune.
In shadows deep, where dreams reside,
We craft the vows that will abide.

Each sentence penned in honest care,
A testament of love we share.
With trembling hands, we rewrite fate,
Each line a chance to celebrate.

The rhythm of each heartbeat sways,
In the warmth of time's embrace.
Together, we will weave anew,
The promises of me and you.

With every breath, we claim our mark,
In love's own light, we leave a spark.
Rewritten words, a journey starts,
Forever bound, our hopeful hearts.

The Canvas of Affection

Brush strokes dance in vibrant hues,
Telling tales of love we choose.
Each color drips, a story flows,
On canvas where true passion grows.

In soft pastels and bold demand,
We paint our dreams with heart and hand.
Shadows whisper secrets deep,
In every layer, memories keep.

A splash of joy, a hint of pain,
Every struggle etched, every gain.
The masterpiece we strive to make,
A legacy that will not shake.

In tender strokes, our lives entwine,
A gallery of moments, divine.
Each brush a heartbeat, each line a sigh,
Together we create, you and I.

The canvas waits for love's embrace,
To capture time, to fix a place.
In every color, our hearts are free,
A work of art, the best of we.

Transformation Through Trust

In shadows cast by doubt's retreat,
We build a bridge, our hearts can meet.
Through winding paths, we grow and learn,
Trusting the fire, as embers burn.

Each step we take, a leap of faith,
In each other's arms, we both find grace.
The scars we bear, they tell a tale,
Of strength and love that will not fail.

With open hearts, we face the night,
The darkness fades, love brings the light.
In vulnerability, we expose our truths,
Together we see, joy becomes our roots.

The tapestry we weave is strong,
In trust, we find where we belong.
Each thread a promise, vibrant and clear,
A bond unbroken, steadfast and near.

Together we rise, hand in hand,
In love's embrace, we take a stand.
Transformation blooms, and in it, we find,
A journey of hearts, forever entwined.

The Solace of Kindred Spirits

In silent nights, we find our way,
Two souls entwined, in shadows play.
With gentle words, we share our cries,
A bond that's forged as time replies.

Through laughter shared, and tears we weep,
In every secret, trust we keep.
In mirrored dreams, our hopes align,
A sacred space that feels divine.

With every glance, our hearts convey,
A language spoken without delay.
In quiet moments, love's embrace,
Defines the beauty of our grace.

Together we rise, with courage bold,
In life's great tale, our story told.
Amidst the storms, we learn to stand,
United in faith, hand in hand.

As kindred spirits, we grow bright,
A constellation in the night.
With every heartbeat, strong and true,
The solace found in me and you.

Embracing the Dawn of Rebirth

In tender light, a day is born,
New dreams awaken, hope adorns.
With each soft ray that graces skin,
A whispered promise deep within.

The past retreats, its shadows fade,
In vibrant hues, new paths are laid.
With open hearts, the world we greet,
Embracing change with steady feet.

The fragrant blooms in morning's breath,
Remind us all of life from death.
With joy we rise, in playful sway,
And dance upon the dawn of day.

Each step we take, a story spun,
As seasons shift, and cycles run.
In harmony, we learn to trust,
In life's great dance, we find our thrust.

So let us greet this blessed morn,
With open arms, our spirits sworn.
To cherish life, with love that swells,
Embracing dawn, where beauty dwells.

Whispers of a Restored Heart

In subtle tones, the heart can sing,
Of love renewed, and joy it brings.
With every beat, a tale retold,
In breaths of warmth, our fears unfold.

Through trials faced, and lessons learned,
A fire within, gently burned.
The scars we bear, a map of grace,
In every line, a sacred space.

With time's embrace, we rise once more,
From ashes deep, our spirits soar.
Each whisper soft, a tender guide,
To lead us on, with love beside.

A heart restored, beats strong and true,
In mirrored depths, we find what's due.
With hands held tight, we walk anew,
In harmony, our souls imbue.

So let the whispers fill the air,
Of love reclaimed, and gentle care.
With every pulse, we start anew,
A journey bright, for me and you.

A Journey of Heartfelt Discovery

With every step, we dare to roam,
In vibrant worlds, we seek our home.
Through valleys deep and mountains high,
We chase the dreams that lift us sky.

With open hearts, we learn to see,
The beauty found in you and me.
In whispered secrets shared at night,
A bond that's forged, forever tight.

The stories told, in laughter shared,
Remind us all of how we cared.
In every smile, a spark ignites,
A journey bright, with endless lights.

Through storms we face, and sunlight's grace,
We find our rhythm, set our pace.
In discoveries, we learn and grow,
With every touch, a deeper flow.

So let us wander, hand in hand,
In every moment, love will stand.
With open hearts, we dare to dream,
A journey birthed from hope's bright beam.

Harmonizing Hearts

In the quiet dawn, we find our way,
Melodies entwined, in light of day.
Every heartbeat sings a sacred tune,
Binding souls as softly as the moon.

Hands held tightly, side by side,
Together we walk, in love we confide.
Through storms of doubt and waves of fear,
Our harmony grows, ever sincere.

Whispers of joy, dancing on the breeze,
Creating a rhythm that always pleases.
In laughter and tears, we play our parts,
The symphony crafted from our hearts.

With every sunset, a promise we make,
To cherish the bond, never to break.
In the tapestry of life, we sew,
Threads of trust that gently flow.

So let our song ring through the night,
A chorus of love, pure and bright.
In this dance of hearts, we can see,
The beauty of love setting us free.

The Echo of Togetherness

In the heart of silence, whispers bloom,
Echoes of laughter dispel the gloom.
When shadows fall, we stand as one,
Together we shine like the morning sun.

Paths intertwined, journeys we share,
In every moment, a breath of care.
With open arms, we welcome the day,
The echo of love guiding our way.

Through valleys low and mountains high,
With each step forward, we reach for the sky.
In the gentle breeze, our spirits soar,
Together we find what we're searching for.

Boundless dreams whispered in the night,
Carved by our hopes, a shared delight.
In unity's strength, we find our grace,
The echo of togetherness, our sacred place.

Though time may pass, and seasons change,
Our bond remains, ever profound, never strange.
In the tapestry woven, one thread, one soul,
Together forever, we become whole.

Stitches of Tomorrow

With needle and thread, we mend the seams,
Stitching our hopes, weaving our dreams.
In the fabric of life, we find our place,
Creating a future, filled with grace.

Each stitch a promise, each knot a vow,
Building the bridge from then to now.
With love as our guide, we forge ahead,
In the pattern of life, no word left unsaid.

Through trials faced, and lessons learned,
In the warmth of connection, our hearts have burned.
Together we craft a story so bright,
Stitches of tomorrow, woven in light.

In moments of doubt, we hold our thread tight,
Walking together, through day and night.
Each line a chapter, each twist a path,
In this beautiful quilt, we find our laugh.

So here's to the future, a vibrant design,
With threads of togetherness, yours and mine.
In every stitch, a piece of our souls,
Stitches of tomorrow, as time kindly rolls.

The Revival of Our Essence

In the still of the night, a spark ignites,
A whisper of hope in the darkest sights.
The essence within begins to rise,
In the quiet moments, truth never lies.

From ashes of doubt, the flame does grow,
Reviving the spirit, with every glow.
In the dance of renewal, we find our way,
Together we'll shine, come what may.

Like blossoms in spring, we break through the ground,
Reclaiming our joy, where love is found.
With every breath, we spark the fire,
The revival of essence, our hearts' desire.

Through trials faced, strength we gain,
In unity's power, we break every chain.
In the tapestry woven, vibrant and bright,
The revival of our essence, a beacon of light.

So let us awaken, with passion and grace,
Embracing the journey, let love take its place.
In the rhythm of life, we rise and we sing,
The revival of essence, in the joy it brings.

Foundations of Belonging

In shadows cast by ancient trees,
We find our roots beneath the leaves.
A circle formed of hearts so free,
Together, holding what we believe.

Through laughter shared and sorrows too,
We build a bridge that feels like home.
With every word, a bond anew,
A tapestry of love we roam.

Each story woven, thread by thread,
Connects the souls that walk this earth.
In every tear, in every spread,
We find the joy of shared rebirth.

In whispered dreams, our hopes unfold,
Embracing differences so bright.
In unity, our hearts turn bold,
Creating love that shines like light.

Together, here, we stand as one,
Defying trials that come our way.
In every dusk, we greet the sun,
Foundations strong, come what may.

Cadence of Healing

In gentle rhythms, time does bend,
A melody that softly calls.
With every sigh, the heart can mend,
In whispers sweet, the spirit falls.

Through valleys low, where shadows creep,
As dawn unveils its warming grace.
The wounds may ache, yet hope we keep,
In every tear, we find our place.

The pulse of life beats on and on,
Each moment teaches us to grow.
From fragments lost, new paths are drawn,
In silent strength, we learn to flow.

Embracing scars, we wear them proud,
A badge of stories lived and told.
United under one large shroud,
In unity, our hearts consoled.

As nature turns, we bloom again,
With every breeze, we feel the change.
In cycles deep, our joy will reign,
The cadence sweet, it feels so strange.

Whispers of Restoration

From ashes rise the dreams unsaid,
In quiet spaces, life renews.
The earth breathes deep, where hope has bled,
In whispers soft, a love imbues.

With every dawn, a promise made,
To heal the wounds and mend the seams.
In every light, the shadows fade,
As kindred spirits chase their dreams.

Beneath the moon, we find our peace,
In sacred moments shared with love.
Where sorrows fade, the joys increase,
And all that's lost is found above.

With gentle hands, we weave the days,
Creating tapestries of light.
In every breath, the spirit plays,
Restoring hearts, dispelling night.

Together, we embrace the change,
With open arms and open hearts.
In whispers soft, we find the range,
Of what it means to heal in parts.

In the Embrace of Tenderness

In soft embraces, hearts unwind,
With every hug, a warmth takes flight.
In gentle words, our love defined,
We find our way through darkest night.

With quiet strength, we face the storms,
As every tear brings us to breath.
In kindness wrapped, our spirit warms,
In tender space, we conquer death.

Through starlit skies, we walk as one,
With hands entwined, a sacred bond.
In every loss, new battles won,
In tenderness, of each response.

Through laughter bright and silence shared,
We build a world that lifts us high.
In softest glances, we have dared,
To open wide our hearts and fly.

Together in this blessed grace,
We journey forth, come what may bring.
In life's embrace, we find our place,
In tenderness, our spirits sing.

The Sunshine After the Rain

Clouds drift away, the sky turns bright,
Raindrops sparkle in the warm sunlight.
Colors blossom, fresh scents in the air,
Nature smiles, a beautiful affair.

A rainbow arches, a promise anew,
Whispers of hope in every hue.
The world is washed, reborn with grace,
In every corner, there's a smiling face.

Children laugh, splashing in puddles,
Joy unfurling amid the cuddles.
Life's rhythms dance, a gentle refrain,
Hearts rejoice in the warm after the rain.

With every drop, the earth finds its tune,
Under the glow of a bright, shining moon.
Tomorrow holds wonders, an open door,
A melody sweet that we can't ignore.

So embrace the sun, let the light in,
Chase away shadows and let life begin.
In the stillness, find what remains,
The sunshine comes after all the rains.

Reverberations of a Tender Heart

In the quiet depths, where emotions stir,
The echoes of love, a gentle murmur.
Every heartbeat whispers your name,
In the silence, there's no shame.

Soft reflections in a lover's gaze,
A dance so sweet, it sets us ablaze.
Tender moments caught in time,
Creating memories, a rhythm, a rhyme.

Through trials faced, we grow and bend,
In this embrace, there's no end.
Reverberations of souls intertwined,
In the fabric of love, peace we find.

Every tear shed, a story unfolds,
Through joy and sorrow, our bond molds.
Let the heart sing, let feelings flow,
In this harmony, we continue to grow.

With each touch, a spark ignites,
In the warmth of love, we find our lights.
So hold me close, let life unfurl,
Together we dance in this tender swirl.

Finding Home in Your Stillness

In your gentle gaze, I find my place,
A refuge sweet, a warm embrace.
Like the calm sea, so wide and deep,
In your stillness, my soul can weep.

Whispers of silence, a sacred bond,
In each heartbeat, our dreams respond.
Time pauses, the world fades away,
In this moment, forever we stay.

Here lies the solace, where shadows cease,
In your presence, I discover peace.
With every breath, the echoes align,
In your stillness, I know you're mine.

Beneath the stars, we sit hand in hand,
No need for words, we understand.
In the quietude, our hearts unite,
Finding home in this soft twilight.

So let the chaos race and roar,
In your stillness, I need no more.
Wrapped in love, we quietly sway,
Finding home, come what may.

A Chorus of Resounding Affections

In the air, a melody flows,
A chorus of love that only grows.
Voices join in sweet harmony,
Singing softly, you and me.

Notes of laughter, whispers of care,
Every heartbeat, a song we share.
With every verse, our stories blend,
A symphony that will never end.

Moments captured, like stars in the night,
Illuminating the path, shining bright.
Together we dream, our spirits soar,
In this chorus, we ask for more.

Through trials faced and rivers crossed,
In this song, there's never a loss.
Love's refrain lifts us high,
Creating echoes that reach the sky.

So sing with me, through joy and strife,
In this harmony, we find our life.
With every note that we express,
A chorus of love, we truly bless.

Surrendering to Serenity

In the quiet of the dawn,
Whispers of the heart abide.
Gentle waves upon the shore,
Embrace the peace inside.

Leaves that dance upon the breeze,
Softly beckon, letting go.
Each moment, like a sigh,
Reminds us on this flow.

Casting doubts into the void,
Finding stillness in the here.
In the silence, echoes play,
Trust the path, release your fear.

Clouds may drift, yet sun will shine,
In the depths of every trial.
Breathe in love, exhale the strife,
Surrender, find your smile.

As the stars embrace the night,
Our souls entwined in light's embrace.
Let the journey lead us home,
To the heart of endless space.

Mosaic of Togetherness

In a garden, colors bloom,
Scattered pieces find their place.
Every heart a vibrant note,
Joining in this warm embrace.

Hands that weave through laughter's thread,
Creating bonds that time won't sever.
With every shared and whispered word,
We stitch a life of dreams forever.

Each day dawns with painted skies,
A tapestry of moments bright.
In unity, we paint our path,
Together, chasing morning light.

Through the storms and into rain,
We rise, a chorus in the fall.
Our strength is love, a guiding flame,
Holding each, we stand tall.

Let the world unfold with grace,
For in our hearts, we all belong.
A mosaic of every soul,
In harmony, we sing our song.

Illuminated by Connection

Beneath the sky, two paths converge,
With eyes that speak in silent ways.
In the quiet, hearts ignite,
Kindred spirits in the haze.

Every laughter, every tear,
Echoes in the space between.
A dance of souls across the night,
Where light and love are seen.

In shared stories, bridges form,
Weaving tales of joy and strife.
From whispered hopes, new dreams arise,
Igniting fire to life.

Though miles may stretch, we're tethered tight,
Invisible threads of trust remain.
In every heartbeat, there's a light,
A bond, transcending pain.

Together, we illuminate,
The shadows lurking in our fears.
As one, we shine, unbroken, bright,
In connection, love appears.

Fragments into Wholeness

Scattered pieces on the floor,
Each shard a tale of days gone past.
In the mess, there's beauty found,
Transformation shapes the cast.

With gentle hands, we mend the cracks,
As sunlight filters through the gloom.
Every flaw speaks to the truth,
That life is art, amidst the room.

In the dance of broken dreams,
We find the strength to rise anew.
With every heartbeat, we compose,
A symphony, fresh and true.

Whispers of the past remind,
That healing takes both time and grace.
From fragments, we will form the whole,
And every scar, a sacred space.

We gather moments, piece by piece,
An exquisite mosaic of the heart.
With love as glue, we find our way,
In wholeness, we're no longer apart.

Threads of Resilience

In the weave of life, we find our grace,
Every thread tells a tale, a soft embrace.
Strength in the fibers, enduring and true,
Together we rise, as we break through.

Through storms and shadows, we forge our way,
With colors of courage that never sway.
Each knot a reminder of battles we face,
Unraveling fears, finding our place.

In the fabric of life, we stitch our dreams,
Every seam a promise, or so it seems.
Together we gather, in love we reside,
Threads of resilience, forever our guide.

As time unravels, we learn to mend,
With threads of compassion, our hearts we blend.
Through trials we grow, side by side we stand,
In the tapestry of life, hand in hand.

So let us embrace the journey ahead,
With threads of resilience, our spirits fed.
Together we'll weave a story so bright,
In the warmth of our bonds, we find the light.

The Art of Letting In

Open the door to the heart's soft glow,
Invite the warmth of love to flow.
With each gentle breath, we shed the past,
The art of letting in, a spell so cast.

Like petals unfolding in early spring,
We welcome the joys that each moment brings.
In the silence of trust, we find our way,
To let in the light of a brand new day.

Breathe in the fragrance of hope's embrace,
In the dance of connection, we find our place.
With courage we stand, vulnerabilities bare,
The art of letting in, a fragile affair.

With every heartbeat, we learn to share,
The weight of our burdens, the love we declare.
Not just for ourselves, but for those we hold dear,
Embracing the journey, casting out fear.

So let us cherish the bonds we create,
The art of letting in, a beautiful fate.
In the tapestry of life, we find our thread,
Through love and acceptance, our spirits are fed.

A Journey Through Forgiveness

In the quiet of night, a whisper remains,
Forgiveness, a journey that often contains.
Steps taken slowly, as hearts mend and heal,
Releasing the burdens, allowing us to feel.

Through valleys of doubt, we traverse the pain,
Each moment a chance to dance in the rain.
With kindness as compass, we navigate strife,
A path towards healing, a celebration of life.

In the mirror of time, reflection we find,
The power of letting go, gentle and kind.
With each act of grace, we tear down the walls,
A journey through forgiveness, answering the calls.

As shadows diminish and light starts to spread,
In the embrace of compassion, our spirits are fed.
With courage as armor, we walk through the gate,
A journey through forgiveness, love conquers hate.

So take my hand gently, let's wander this way,
Together in unity, come what may.
With hearts that are open, our burdens released,
In the journey of forgiveness, we find our peace.

The Palette of Reconciliation

Brush strokes of colors, vivid and bright,
A canvas of moments, waiting for light.
With hues of compassion, we paint the scene,
The palette of reconciliation, serene.

Each color a story, each shade a truth,
In the blend of our hearts, we capture our youth.
Through laughter and sorrow, we wield the brush,
Creating a masterpiece, in harmony's hush.

When differences fade, and understanding grows,
The palette of life, in a beautiful show.
With every new layer, our spirits unite,
In the tapestry woven, we find our delight.

With strokes of forgiveness, the picture expands,
Embracing our flaws, accepting our strands.
Together we color the world that we see,
In the palette of reconciliation, we're free.

So let us gather the hues of our hearts,
Creating connections, as each day starts.
With love as our canvas, and hope as our skill,
In the palette of reconciliation, we fulfill.

Radiant Journeys

In dawn's embrace, we set our course,
With dreams like stars, they guide us forth.
Every step brings new horizons,
Whispers of hope, in the softest light.

Rivers of laughter, through valleys wide,
Mountains of courage, where we abide.
The path unwinds, a tapestry spun,
With each heartbeat, we marvel and run.

Through shadows cast, our spirit soars,
In the dance of fate, we find open doors.
Radiance blooms, in hearts aglow,
On these journeys, we learn to grow.

With every sunset, lessons unfold,
In the twilight's hush, stories told.
Hand in hand, we write our tales,
Onward we wander, as love prevails.

From peaks of joy, to valleys deep,
Promises made, in moments we keep.
Radiant journeys, forever entwined,
In the book of life, true treasures we find.

The Alchemy of Emotions

In shadows bright, feelings ignite,
A pot of gold, within the night.
Laughter and tears, a blend so rare,
The colors of life, in moments we share.

Heartbeats echo, in the silence profound,
Transformation waits, in the depths unbound.
Joy turns to sorrow, then back again,
A dance of light, like the sun and rain.

Each pulse a potion, crafted with care,
Alchemy's magic, in the open air.
Love's gentle touch, the fiercest flame,
In every whisper, we feel the same.

Moments in bloom, a fragrant surprise,
Awakening senses, opening eyes.
In the heart's chamber, emotions collide,
A tapestry woven, with threads of pride.

With time as the teacher, we learn to bend,
The art of release, a way to mend.
In every heartbeat, we find our part,
The alchemy of emotions, a work of art.

In the Arms of Time

Embraced by hours, we drift and sway,
Moments unravel, like clouds in play.
Each tick a whisper, soft and true,
Guiding our journey, in shades of blue.

From dawn to dusk, the stories unfold,
In the warmth of presence, memories hold.
Time is a river, flowing so free,
Cradling lives, like leaves on a spree.

In laughter's echo, in silence's sigh,
We find our meaning, as days slip by.
The dance of seasons, a waltz divine,
Forever tethered, in the arms of time.

With every heartbeat, a new grace appears,
The essence of love, through laughter and tears.
Moments like pearls, strung one by one,
In the arms of time, we've just begun.

A tapestry woven, of dreams and fate,
In the gentle embrace, we celebrate.
Here in this moment, we find our rhyme,
Eternally cherished, in the arms of time.

The Cultivation of Joy

In gardens of hope, we sow our dreams,
With seeds of laughter, in sunlit beams.
Every smile nurtured, blossoms in grace,
A tapestry brightens, in this sacred space.

From sunlight's touch, to the rain's soft kiss,
We cultivate joy, in moments like this.
The fragrance of kindness, wafts in the air,
In the dance of living, we're blissfully bare.

With hands intertwined, we dig deep and true,
In the rich soil of love, our spirits renew.
Tending the roots of what we hold dear,
In every heartbeat, our purpose is clear.

Through the seasons that change, we find our way,
In the light of each dawn, we gather and play.
The bloom of tomorrow, a promise in sight,
The cultivation of joy, our eternal light.

With each passing day, gratitude blooms,
Filling our hearts and dispelling the glooms.
In life's gentle rhythm, we find sweet employ,
In cultivating love, we harvest our joy.

Echoes of Comforting Silence

In the stillness, whispers fade,
Beneath the trees, shadows wade.
Gentle breezes cool the air,
Wrapped in peace, without a care.

Moments linger, soft and bright,
Fading stars in the quiet night.
Heartbeat steady, mind at ease,
Silent thoughts drift like the breeze.

In the calm, a soothing balm,
Nature's heartbeat, pure and calm.
Every sigh, a soft embrace,
Comfort found in sacred space.

Voices murmur in the dark,
Fleeting sparks, a tiny spark.
Memory's echo leads the way,
Guiding hearts in disarray.

Silence speaks, a tender song,
Where the weary all belong.
In its depths, we find our grace,
Echoes of love's warm embrace.

Blooming Beyond the Barricades

In cracked concrete, flowers rise,
Petals bright against the skies.
Colors clash, yet softly blend,
Strength emerges, hearts unbend.

Walls may rise, but dreams will soar,
Roots break through, forevermore.
With every bud, a silent roar,
Life insists, it must explore.

Sunlight kisses every leaf,
Hope bursts forth, beyond the grief.
Nature's will cannot be tamed,
Through the cracks, love is named.

Wind may howl, and storms may fight,
Yet blooms know how to seek the light.
In every struggle, unity found,
A tapestry grows from the ground.

Together they stand, hand in hand,
Defying odds, they make their stand.
In vibrant hues, they claim their fate,
Blooming strong, never too late.

The Taste of Sweet Renewal

Fresh dawn breaks with golden rays,
Softly chasing night away.
A sip of warmth, the sun bestows,
On tired souls, as daylight glows.

Tears of rain kiss the earth,
Life awakens, senses mirth.
Every blade, a dance anew,
In the glow, the world feels true.

Beneath the soil, life hides deep,
Promises made, secrets keep.
Fruits of labor, flavors burst,
In every moment, joy immersed.

Breath of spring, the air is sweet,
Filling hearts with rhythmic beat.
Every taste, a story spun,
A cycle rich, where all is one.

In the essence of each bite,
We find the love, pure and bright.
With every turn, we rise and fall,
The taste of life, nurturing all.

Hands Held Through the Fog

Through the mist, our fingers clasp,
Silent strength in every grasp.
Hearts aligned where shadows play,
Together we'll find our way.

Veils of gray, the world obscured,
Yet with you, my heart's assured.
In the haze, we navigate,
Holding tight to love's estate.

Every step, a cautious tread,
Yet with you, there's no dread.
In the unknown, trust will grow,
Brighter paths begin to show.

Waves of doubt may crash and swell,
But in your eyes, I find my well.
Every tender squeeze says more,
Together we can face the core.

As the fog begins to clear,
I find courage, you are near.
Hand in hand, we break the spell,
A radiant light, where hope can dwell.

Comfort in a Knowing Gaze

In the silence, eyes connect,
Whispers linger, hearts reflect.
A glance that speaks of understanding,
In that gaze, love is expanding.

No need for words, we both just know,
A gentle warmth begins to flow.
Through storms and shadows, side by side,
A knowing glance, our hearts abide.

In moments small, our souls entwined,
In every gaze, a truth defined.
We find our peace within each stare,
A bond unbroken, always there.

Through trials faced, we stand so strong,
Each silent look, a subtle song.
With every blink, we share our fate,
In that gaze, we cultivate.

So when the world feels cold and bleak,
Your knowing eyes, the strength I seek.
In every glance, a soft embrace,
Together, we find our sacred space.

Falling Like Leaves into Your Embrace

Each autumn leaf, a journey's end,
Soft whispers as the seasons blend.
I feel your warmth, my heart takes flight,
Wrapped in love, we chase the light.

Falling gently, the world in hues,
A tapestry of reds and blues.
In every rustle, a soft sigh,
Into your arms, I long to fly.

As branches sway, the breezes call,
I find my home within your thrall.
The ground below, so cool and wide,
Together, we'll dance, side by side.

Like whispers shared in quiet woods,
We cultivate these tender buds.
With every fall, we rise anew,
Your gentle arms, my skies of blue.

When winter comes to claim the day,
I'll find my comfort in your sway.
Falling like leaves, we intertwine,
In every season, you are mine.

Sunrise After the Longest Night

In the depths of dark despair,
Hope flickers, fragile, rare.
Yet dawn breaks bright, a golden ray,
Chasing shadows far away.

The night may stretch, unyielding, long,
But in my heart, there stirs a song.
With every moment, hope ignites,
A symphony of vibrant lights.

The mountains gleam in morning's glow,
A promise whispered soft and slow.
In hues of pink, the world awakes,
A canvas bright, love overtakes.

As day unfolds, my spirit soars,
The weight of night no longer wars.
For every struggle, love's embrace,
Transcends the pain, and finds its place.

So here I stand, with heart ablaze,
In the light of dawn, I sing your praise.
Together, facing what's in sight,
We rise anew, from longest night.

A Melody of Trust Restored

In quiet chords, our hearts align,
A symphony of love divine.
Through trials faced, we found our way,
In every note, our spirits play.

With gentle rhythms, life renews,
A song of hope that guides us through.
Each whispered word, a healing balm,
Together, we remain so calm.

The echoes of the past may fade,
But in this moment, trust is made.
A tender harmony unfolds,
In every silence, truth upholds.

As melodies weave through dusk and dawn,
We find our place where we belong.
With every breath, the music grows,
In heartbeats shared, our love bestows.

So let us dance through every storm,
In trust restored, our hearts are warm.
In this duet, forever bound,
A perfect love, forever found.

Petals on the Path of Healing

Gentle whispers in the breeze,
Petals drift from ancient trees.
Every step, a soft embrace,
Nature sings of hope and grace.

Sunlight breaks through clouds of gray,
Warming hearts that lost their way.
Fragments mend with tender care,
Love's sweet fragrance fills the air.

Every tear that falls like rain,
Nurtures growth from endless pain.
On this path, each scar will bloom,
Finding light, dispelling gloom.

In the gardens of our mind,
Beauty grows, and strength we find.
Through the storms, we dance and sway,
Healing guides us day by day.

Together hand in hand, we tread,
Petals scatter, words unsaid.
On this journey, hope remains,
Life renews through love's refrains.

Healing Waters of Togetherness

In a stream where dreams take flight,
Waves of laughter shine so bright.
Hearts entwined, a sacred bond,
In this flow, we are beyond.

Every ripple tells a tale,
Shared joys that will never pale.
As the waters gently weave,
Strength we find, we do believe.

When we gather by the shore,
Silent hopes and dreams we pour.
In this place where souls unite,
Healing blooms, and fears take flight.

Raindrops dance upon our skin,
Washing doubts and fears within.
Together strong, we face the tide,
In this love, we will abide.

Let the currents guide our way,
Through life's storms, we'll gently sway.
In the waters of our hearts,
Healing begins, and love imparts.

In the Garden of Gentle Hearts

Among the blossoms, soft and rare,
Gentle souls that find their care.
In this garden, love will thrive,
Nurtured by the will to strive.

Each petal tells a story sweet,
Of kindness found in hearts that meet.
Roots entwined beneath the soil,
Fostering growth through patient toil.

In the quiet moments shared,
Tender glances, hopes declared.
From the earth, our spirits rise,
Reaching ever for the skies.

With every season's soft embrace,
We discover our own place.
In this haven, dreams take flight,
Hearts converge in pure delight.

Together in this sacred space,
Finding warmth, a gentle grace.
In the garden, love will bloom,
Filling all with sweet perfume.

A Portrait of Whimsical Trust

In colors bold, a canvas bright,
Trust takes shape in morning light.
Every stroke, a story spun,
Whimsy dances, hearts are one.

With laughter's brush, we draw the dreams,
Splashing joy in vibrant streams.
In this art, no fear to face,
Creativity finds its place.

Through playful forms, we learn to see,
The beauty in our unity.
A gentle touch, a knowing glance,
In this portrait, we find chance.

Lines entwined, we sketch the past,
Moments cherished, shadows cast.
With each hue, our spirits free,
Whimsy blooms in harmony.

A masterpiece of hearts aligned,
In this canvas, love defined.
Together here, we trust and play,
In this art, we find our way.

Finding Solace in Your Voice

In whispers soft like summer rain,
I find the calm amidst the pain.
Your voice, a balm for weary days,
Guides me through the shadowed maze.

Each note a thread, woven with care,
A song that lingers in the air.
In echoes rich, I lose and find,
A peace that bridges heart and mind.

When silence reigns and doubts arise,
Your laughter lifts me to the skies.
In every chord, I hear the light,
That leads me home through darkest night.

Though distance stretches like the sea,
Your words still carry close to me.
In every syllable, love's embrace,
I find my refuge, my sacred space.

So let the world grow dim and wide,
Your voice remains, my trusted guide.
In each refrain, my spirit soars,
Finding solace forevermore.

The Canvas of Tomorrow's Promise

Brush strokes of hope on a blank slate,
Each hue whispers of a fate.
With every color, dreams ignite,
Painting visions bathed in light.

The dawn unfolds a tender tale,
As visions rise, I cannot fail.
In every shade, a chance to grow,
The canvas blooms as futures flow.

With each decision, a mark I leave,
Promises linger, every weave.
A tapestry of chance and strife,
Threads of courage, threads of life.

As night approaches with its hue,
I trust the dawn will bring what's new.
Hope's vibrant glow will guide my way,
Crafting dreams in the light of day.

So let me paint with heart and fire,
The masterpiece of my desire.
With passion bold, I dance and strive,
The canvas holds the will to thrive.

Traces of Radiance in the Dark

In shadows deep where silence sighs,
A flicker glows, a spark replies.
Amidst the gloom, hope dares to gleam,
Whispering softly, life's sweet dream.

The night enfolds with tender arms,
Yet in its depths, a light still charms.
Each star a promise, shining bright,
Guiding lost souls through endless night.

With every breath, I feel the grace,
Of radiant traces in this space.
In darkened realms, beauty finds way,
To cradle hearts that long to stay.

So let the shadows come and play,
I'll seek the light in night's ballet.
For in the dark, I learn to see,
The traces of what's meant to be.

Embrace the night, it won't despair,
For even dark can hold a flare.
In every corner, whispers start,
Traces of love, a shining heart.

Cradled by Endless Affection

In tender arms, I find my rest,
The warmth of love, a soothing nest.
Each heartbeat sings a lullaby,
Cradled by dreams that soar and fly.

Through gentle tides of life we sail,
With you, my compass, I prevail.
In every touch, a promise waits,
Affection blooms, and joy elates.

Your laughter dances in the air,
A melody beyond compare.
In every glance, a spark ignites,
Cradled in love, my spirit lights.

As seasons change and years unfold,
Our story writes in threads of gold.
With every memory, woven tight,
Endless affection, our heart's delight.

So let the world around us spin,
In your embrace, I always win.
For time may pass and shadows grow,
Cradled in love, I always know.

Beyond the Pain

In shadows deep, where silence dwells,
The heartache lingers, softly swells.
Yet dawn breaks through, with gentle light,
Hope whispers softly, guiding the night.

With tender strength, we rise again,
Embracing wounds, we find our kin.
Each scar a story, woven tight,
Forging paths from dark to bright.

The tears we've shed, now pearls of grace,
In every loss, we've found our place.
Together we stand, hand in hand,
Beyond the pain, together we band.

With every breath, we find our way,
Through storms of doubt, we'll choose to stay.
Resilience blooms, a steadfast flower,
Beyond the pain, we reclaim our power.

So here's to hope, let it ignite,
The journey holds both dark and light.
With hearts aligned, we'll brave the rain,
And dance beneath the sun again.

A Whisper

In the stillness, secrets hum,
Soft as shadows, dreams become.
A fleeting thought, a gentle sigh,
In whispered tones, we learn to fly.

The world can hush, yet voices speak,
In quiet moments, strong yet meek.
The heart knows truths, long laid to rest,
In whispers soft, we are all blessed.

Through tangled paths, we search for light,
A single whisper ignites the night.
In echoes faint, our hopes revive,
In whispered love, we feel alive.

The space between, where silence grows,
Allows the heart to freely pose.
In whispers dear, we find our song,
Together we dance, where we belong.

So take a moment, breathe it in,
The whispered world waits to begin.
In every breath, let love persist,
In tender whispers, we coexist.

Fostering Hope with Each Step

With every step, the path unfolds,
A journey brave, our hearts behold.
In every tread, a dream we chase,
Fostering hope, we find our place.

Beneath the weight of doubt and fear,
The light of courage draws us near.
We walk the lines of joy and grief,
In every heartbeat, we find belief.

Hand in hand, we face the climb,
In unified grace, we weave through time.
Together we rise, with spirits free,
Fostering hope — the best we can be.

Through valleys low and mountains steep,
Our dreams take flight, as shadows creep.
Each step a whisper, each pause a chance,
In hope's embrace, we learn to dance.

So take a breath, and mark the space,
With every step, embrace the grace.
For in the journey, we truly grow,
Fostering hope, we let love flow.

Echoes of Unfurling Trust

In shadows cast, where secrets lie,
The heart beats softly, a quiet cry.
Each echo whispers, soft and low,
Trust unfurls, like flowers in snow.

Breaking walls built high and strong,
Together we sing our brave new song.
With every step, we learn to see,
The power found in you and me.

In the circle of time, we share our fears,
And in our laughter, the pain disappears.
We weave our stories, thread by thread,
In echoes of trust, our spirits are fed.

Beneath the stars, our dreams ignite,
With open hearts, we embrace the night.
Hand in hand, we face what's true,
In echoes of trust, we start anew.

So take a leap, let courage bloom,
In the garden of hope, we'll chase the gloom.
For in the trust, we lay our claim,
Echoes resound, together the same.

The Journey Toward Wholeness

In scattered pieces, we start to mend,
Each fragment tells a tale, my friend.
With every step, we breathe anew,
The journey unfolds, a path so true.

Through winding roads, we find our way,
The heart's resilience guides each day.
In every stumble, we learn to rise,
Woven in courage, we find the skies.

Connected hearts, we weave our dreams,
In unity's light, we share our themes.
With open arms, we greet the change,
The journey toward wholeness, never strange.

So here we stand, with wounds embraced,
In love's vast journey, we find our place.
Together we walk, hand in hand,
The journey toward wholeness, brightly planned.

Let time be grace, let love be our guide,
For in this journey, we shall confide.
In every moment, we learn and grow,
The journey toward wholeness, let it flow.

Milton Keynes UK
Ingram Content Group UK Ltd.
UKHW022119251124
451529UK00012B/606